Taiwan

by Heather DiLorenzo Williams

Consultant: Marjorie Faulstich Orellana, PhD
Professor of Urban Schooling
University of California, Los Angeles

BEARPORT
PUBLISHING

New York, New York

Credits

Cover, © imtmphoto/iStock and © PatrickStedrak/iStock; TOC, © chatuphot/Shutterstock; 4, © Sean Pavone/Shutterstock; 5T, © CHEN MIN CHUN/Shutterstock; 5B, © HTU/Shutterstock; 7, © asiastock/Shutterstock; 8, © Chen Liang-Dao/Shutterstock; 9, © FenlioQ/Shutterstock; 10, © asiastock/Shutterstock; 11, © feathercollector/Shutterstock; 12, © Perry Svensson/Alamy Stock Photo; 13, © Charlesimage/Shutterstock; 15, © Perry Svensson/Alamy; 16, © Denys Bogdanov/Shutterstock; 17, © michaeljung/Shutterstock; 18, © GoranQ/iStock; 19, © 2p2play/Shutterstock; 20, © Jeffrey Liao/Shutterstock; 21, © ESB Professional/Shutterstock; 22, © r.nagy/Shutterstock; 23T, © EQRoy/Shutterstock; 23B, © JEEPNEX/Shutterstock; 24, © TK Kurikawa/Shutterstock; 24T, © FenlioQ/Shutterstock; 25, © weniliou/Shutterstock; 26, © AJ_Watt/iStock; 26B, © wu hsiung/Shutterstock; 27T, © glen photo/Shutterstock; 27B, © Makistock/Shutterstock; 28–29, © Shi Yali/Shutterstock; 29, © Aneta Lysakova/Shutterstock; 30T, © robtxek/Shutterstock and © Avigator Thailand/Shutterstock; 30B, © Robert CHG/Shutterstock; 31 (T to B), © FenlioQ/Shutterstock, © Perry Svensson/Alamy, © Perry Svensson/Alamy, © lavizzara/Shutterstock, © Shi Yali/Shutterstock, and © Jeffrey Liao/Shutterstock; 32, © Kiev.Victor/Shutterstock.

Publisher: Kenn Goin
Senior Editor: Joyce Tavolacci
Creative Director: Spencer Brinker
Design: Debrah Kaiser
Photo Researcher: Book Buddy Media

Library of Congress Cataloging-in-Publication Data

Names: Williams, Heather DiLorenzo, author.
Title: Taiwan / by Heather DiLorenzo Williams.
Description: New York, New York : Bearport Publishing, [2019] | Series:
    Countries we come from | Includes bibliographical references and index.
Identifiers: LCCN 2018044227 (print) | LCCN 2018044966 (ebook) | ISBN
    9781642802603 (ebook) | ISBN 9781642801910 (library binding)
Subjects: LCSH: Taiwan—Juvenile literature.
Classification: LCC DS799 (ebook) | LCC DS799 .W55 2019 (print) | DDC
    951.249—dc23
LC record available at https://lccn.loc.gov/2018044227

For more information, write to Bearport Publishing Company, Inc., 45 West 21st Street, Suite 3B, New York, New York 10010. Printed in the United States of America.

10 9 8 7 6 5 4 3 2 1

Contents

This Is Taiwan

UNIQUE

FUN

Beautiful

Taiwan is a group of islands near China.

Over 23 million people live there!

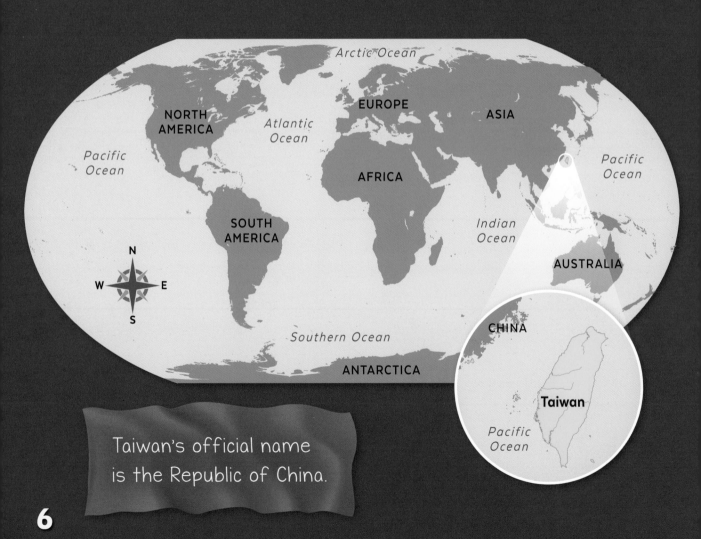

Taiwan's official name is the Republic of China.

Taiwan has many types of land. Beaches surround the island country.

Flat plains cover parts of western Taiwan.

Rugged mountains stretch across the east.

Thick forests cover over half of Taiwan!

9

Amazing animals live in Taiwan's forests.

The macaque (mah-KACK) has big cheeks for holding food.

The Ryukyu (ree-YOU-kyoo) flying fox is a bat that eats fruit.

The Taiwan deer stag beetle has giant mouthparts.

There are 18,000 different kinds of insects in Taiwan!

Taiwan is warm and **humid**.

Summer is **monsoon** season.

Lots of rain falls.

2

Summer is also when typhoons strike.

These big storms bring heavy rain and strong winds.

Many people in Taiwan carry umbrellas. These are used for both the rain and sun!

Over the years, different countries have ruled Taiwan.

China controlled the land for hundreds of years.

Taiwan was once called Formosa, which means "beautiful island."

Today, Taiwan calls itself an **independent** country.

However, China still claims the island.

The main language in Taiwan is Mandarin Chinese.

This is how you say *hello* in Mandarin:

Ni hao
(NEE how)

This is how you say *goodbye*:

Zai jian
(zye JEEY-en)

There are over 10,000 symbols in the Chinese language.

The **capital** of Taiwan is Taipei (tie-PAY).

Taipei is one of the largest cities in Taiwan.

The garbage trucks in Taipei play music. The music tells people to bring their trash outside!

Taiwanese garbage truck

19

Taipei 101 is a huge **skyscraper** in the city.

It was built with extra strong steel.

The building has 101 floors.

It's the eighth-tallest tower in the world!

Taipei 101 lights up a different color each day of the week.

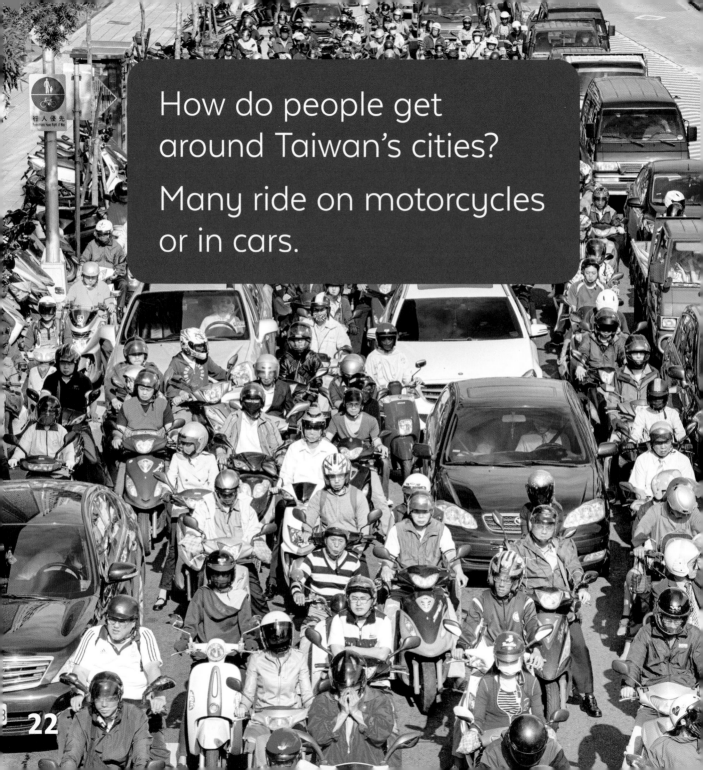

How do people get around Taiwan's cities?

Many ride on motorcycles or in cars.

People also travel by plane
or by super-fast train.

This train travels
186 miles (300 km)
per hour!

An airline in Taiwan
has a special plane.
It has a picture
of Hello Kitty on it.

23

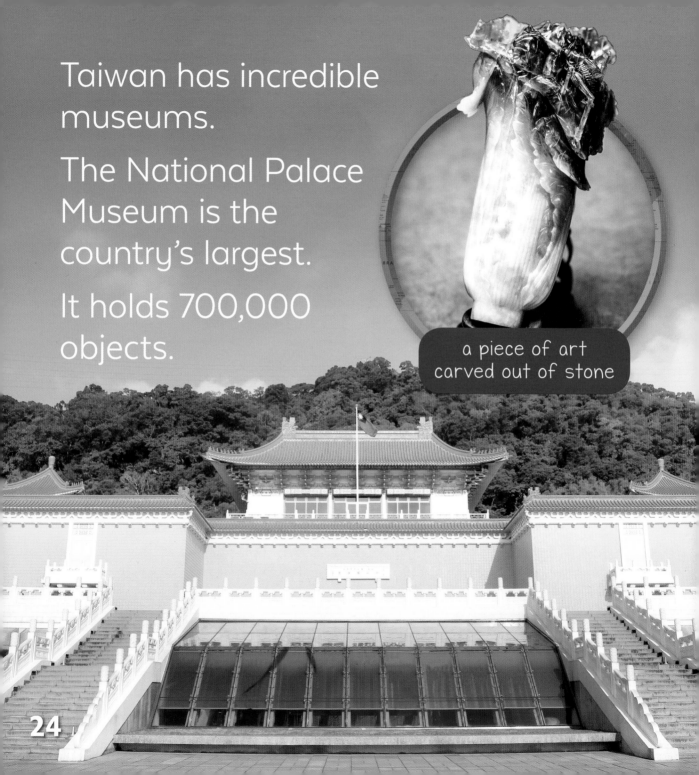

Taiwan has incredible museums.

The National Palace Museum is the country's largest.

It holds 700,000 objects.

a piece of art carved out of stone

The Taiwan Balloons Museum used to be a balloon factory!

Yum! Taiwanese food is tasty.

People enjoy eating seafood, dumplings, and tofu (TOH-foo).

fried tofu

Tofu is made from mashed soybeans.

Taiwan is famous for bubble tea. The "bubbles" are tiny, chewy balls.

People all over Taiwan love baseball.

Taiwan even has its own **professional** baseball league!

Taiwanese people gather each morning to do Tai Chi (TAHY CHEE). It's a type of slow exercise.

Fast Facts

Capital city: Taipei

Population of Taiwan: Over 23 million

Main language: Mandarin Chinese

Money: New Taiwan dollar

Major religions: Taoism and Buddhism

Neighboring countries include: China, Japan, and the Philippines

Cool Fact: The largest statue in Taiwan is 86 feet (26 m) tall!

Glossary

capital (KAP-uh-tuhl) the city where a country's government is based

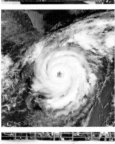

humid (HYOO-med) damp and moist

independent (in-di-PEN-duhnt) free of control by others

monsoon (mon-SOON) strong winds that bring heavy rain

professional (pruh-FESH-uh-nuhl) related to people who are paid to do a job

skyscraper (SKY-skray-per) a very tall building

Index

Read More

Markovics, Joyce. *China (Countries We Come From).* New York: Bearport (2016).

Somervill, Barbara A. *Taiwan (Enchantment of the World).* New York: Children's Press (2014).

Learn More Online

To learn more about Taiwan, visit
www.bearportpublishing.com/CountriesWeComeFrom

About the Author

Heather DiLorenzo Williams lives in North Carolina. She loves reading and traveling to new places.